I0052943

Taste of City Conference 2016 Programme and Abstracts Book

Compiled by Evinç Doğan

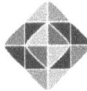

TRANSNATIONAL PRESS LONDON
2016

Taste of City Conference 2016 - Programme and Abstracts Book

Compiled by Evinç Doğan

Copyright © 2016 by Transnational Press London

First Published in 2016 by TRANSNATIONAL PRESS LONDON in the United Kingdom, 12 Ridgeway Gardens, London, N6 5XR, UK.

www.tplondon.com

Paperback

ISBN: 978-1-910781-27-2

Cover Design: Nihal Yazgan | nihalidea.com

Conference website: www.tastecity.net

CONTENT:
SESSIONS AND TIMETABLE

Welcome to Taste of City Conference 2016

1 September 2016 - University of Belgrade, Serbia

Taste of City is an international conference on food and place marketing held at the University of Belgrade, Serbia. The conference focus on food and place marketing, place branding through food and encourage multidisciplinary approaches to place and food marketing and the role and impact of food in marketing and branding of places.

Food and tastes are transferred and transported along the routes of mobility, tourism and connectedness in the era of fast communications and travel. Taste of City Conference 2016 is the first academic research conference with a focus on understanding the dynamics and role of food play in place branding and marketing. Understanding the role of food and taste in forming and reformulating the identity of places, influence of food on the image of cities and countries, changing geographies of food and taste are new avenues for research.

This unique event aims to bring together researchers, scholars and practitioners as well as policy makers to explore the ways in which food is influencing what cities are made up. Hence it touches upon internationalisation strategies, protectionism, interconnectedness, transnational space and marketing, branding, food and taste marketing from a very wide multidisciplinary perspective. All interested academics, students, managers and marketers are invited to this event for exchanging ideas to understand the impact and role of food and to develop appropriate strategies for cities and places in an ever more connected world characterised with supermobility and superdiversity.

I would like to thank all our colleagues who serves on the conference committee, reviewers, authors who also reviewed substantial number of abstracts and papers so far. We thank to the University of Serbia, Faculty of Economics, for hosting and supporting the event. We also thank to our supporters.

Prof Dr Ibrahim Sirkeci
Conference Chair and Professor of Transnational Studies & Marketing | Director of Regent's Centre for Transnational Studies, Faculty of Business and Management, Regent's University London, UK
E-mail: sirkecii@regents.ac.uk
            sirkecii@gmail.com
www.regents.ac.uk/sirkeci
www.tastecity.net

Main Speakers:

Jonathan Liu is Professor of Global Business Management and Faculty research leader. He started his academic career as lecturer at Aston University and moved to Middlesex University as a senior lecturer. In 2002, he became Middlesex University's Professor of Chinese Management, and researched in performance management and managerial development. He joined Newport University in 2006 and was their Associate Dean for Research and Enterprise as well as Professor of Management. Jonathan is the Editor-in-Chief of the *International Journal of Business Performance Management.* He is on the editorial board of the *Journal of Islamic Marketing, Transnational Marketing Journal* and book review editor of the *Journal of Technology Management in China.* Jonathan published over a hundred articles and ten books. Jonathan is on the *Council of the National Conference of Universities Professors,* a Council member of the *Universities China Committee in London.* Jonathan is a trustee and Chairman of the board of the Directors of *Ming-Ai (London) Institute.*

Maktoba Omar is Reader of Marketing Strategy based at Coventry University. Prior to joining Coventry, she worked at Edinburgh Napier University. Dr Omar completed her PhD at the University of Leeds entitled "Contextual Determinants of Standardisation and Entry Strategies in Internationalisation". Since then she has published tens of journal articles and served as editor and referee for a number of academic journals and performed as track chair, presenter and committee member for a number of national and international conferences. She is co-editor of *Transnational Marketing Journal*. She has won the Emerald Literati Network outstanding paper Award in 2008. Currently her main research focus is a study of the impact of branding, emerging markets and foreign direct investment in relation to UK companies. She is a member of a range of professional organisations including the *Academy of Marketing*, the *Academy of International Business* and *the Institute of Learning and Teaching in Higher Education*.

Ibrahim Sirkeci is Ria Professor of Transnational Studies & Marketing and Director of Regent's Centre for Transnational Studies at Regent's University London. Ibrahim Sirkeci received his PhD in Geography in 2003 from the University of Sheffield. Before joining the European Business School London in 2005, he worked at the University of Bristol. His main areas of expertise are remittances, integration, conflict, labour markets, minorities, and segmentation. Sirkeci is known for his work on insecurity and human mobility as well as his conceptual work on culture of migration and conflict model. He has also coined the term "transnational mobile consumers" as he examines connected consumers and the role of mobility in consumer behavior within a transnational marketing context. He is the founding editor of *Transnational Marketing Journal*. His recent books include *Transnational Marketing and Transnational Consumers* (2013, Springer), and *Migration and Remittances during the Global Financial Crisis and Beyond* (2012, World Bank).

Organising Team
CONFERENCE CHAIRS

- ❖ Ibrahim Sirkeci, Regent's University London, United Kingdom
- ❖ Goran Petkovic, University of Belgrade, Serbia

CONFERENCE SCIENTIFIC COMMITTEE

- ❖ Per-Olof Berg, Stockholm University, Sweden
- ❖ Aleksandar Boskovic, University of Belgrade, Serbia
- ❖ Jeffrey H. Cohen, Ohio State University, US
- ❖ Paolo Corvo, University of Gastronomic Sciences, Italy
- ❖ Haris Dajc, University of Belgrade, Serbia
- ❖ John Dawson, University of Edinburgh Business School, UK
- ❖ Evinc Dogan, University of Belgrade, Serbia
- ❖ C. Michael Hall, University of Canterbury, New Zealand
- ❖ Metin Kozak, Dokuz Eylül University, Turkey
- ❖ Robert D. Lemon, University of Heidelberg, Germany
- ❖ Ludovica Leone, University of Bologna, Italy
- ❖ Jonathan Liu, Regent's University London, UK
- ❖ Tamara Ognjevic, Artis Center, ICOM Serbia
- ❖ Maktoba Omar, Coventry University, UK
- ❖ Marc Oliver Opresnik, Lübeck University of Applied Sciences, Germany
- ❖ Goran Petkovic, University of Belgrade, Serbia
- ❖ Jeffrey M. Pilcher, University of Toronto Scarborough, Canada

❖ Aleksandar Radivojevic, University of Belgrade, Serbia

❖ Stefan Rohdewald, Justus-Liebig-Universität, Germany

❖ Paulette Schuster, Open University of Israel, Hebrew University of Jerusalem

❖ Omar Al Serhan, Regent's University London, UK

❖ Dilistan Shipman, Istanbul Bilgi University, Turkey

❖ Ibrahim Sirkeci, Regent's University London, UK

❖ Aleksandra Stupar, University of Belgrade, Serbia

❖ Zafer Yenal, Bogazici University, Turkey

ORGANISING COMMITTEE

❖ Evinç Doğan, FREN, University of Belgrade, Serbia (Manager)

❖ Ibrahim Sirkeci, Faculty of Business and Management, Regent's University London, UK (Chair)

❖ Goran Petkovic, Faculty of Economics, University of Belgrade, Serbia (Co-Chair)

❖ Aleksandar Radivojevic, FREN, University of Belgrade, Serbia

Supporting Organisations

❖ Faculty of Economics & FREN, University of Belgrade, Serbia

❖ Transnational Press London

❖ Transnational Marketing Journal

❖ Border Crossing

Taste of City Conference 2016 Schedule

	1 September - THURSDAY
08:30	REGISTRATION
09.30-11.00	**Opening Plenary Session & Chairs' welcome by** Prof Goran Petkovic, University of Belgrade, Serbia Prof Ibrahim Sirkeci, Regent's University London, UK Prof Jonathan Liu, Regent's University London, UK Dr Maktoba Omar, Coventry University, UK
11:00-11:15	COFFEE BREAK
11:15-12:45	**Parallel Sessions I**
12:45-13:30	LUNCH
13:30-15:00	**Parallel Sessions II**
15:00-15:20	COFFEE BREAK
15:20-16:50	**Parallel Sessions III**
16:50-17:00	COFFEE BREAK
17:00-18:30	**Parallel Sessions IV**
19:30	**CONFERENCE DINNER**

Conference Venue:

Faculty of Economics - University of Belgrade, Kamenicka 6, 11000 Belgrade, Serbia

Taste of City Conference 2016 is hosted by the University of Belgrade, Faculty of Economics, University of Belgrade & FREN (Foundation for the Advancement of Economics) in Belgrade, Serbia. The conference venue is at Faculty of Economics, Kamenicka 6, 11000 Belgrade. Conference venue is quite central and within walking distance of the city centre.

The main rail and bus stations in Belgrade are next to each other, in the centre of Belgrade across the Faculty of Economics.

Belgrade is a relatively big city with good transport system. Belgrade city public transport is provided through a network of bus, trolleybus and tram routes run by GSP "Beograd" and bus services operated by private bus companies. For more information, you can visit the website of Tourist Organisation of Belgrade.

Venue map: Faculty of Economics, Kamenicka 6, Belgrade, Serbia

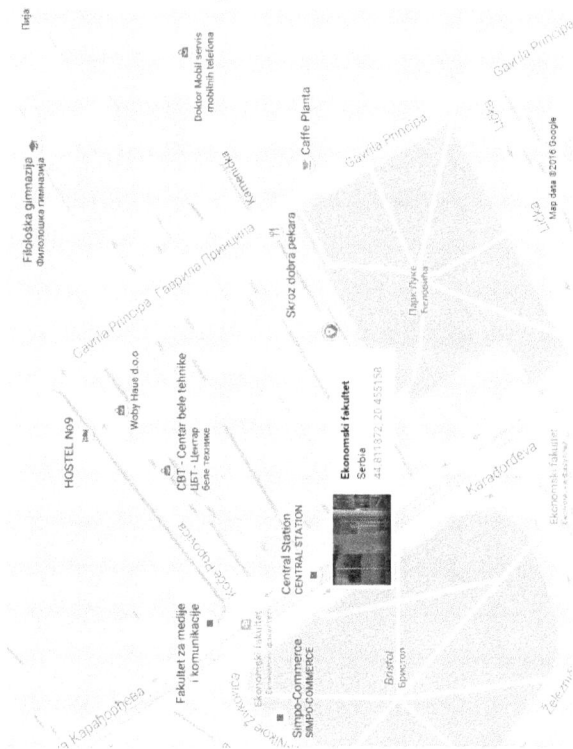

| 08:30-17:00 | **REGISTRATION DESK OPEN** |

| Rectorate Hall |

| 09:30-11:00 | **OPENING PLENARY & WELCOME** |

Welcome by Prof Goran **Petkovic**, Conference Co-Chair, University of Belgrade, Serbia

"Food for Thought – Reflections on the Food Supply Chain and Cities" - Prof Jonathan **Liu**, Regent's University London, UK

"Doner Kebab taking over the UK" - Prof Ibrahim **Sirkeci**, Conference Chair, Regent's University London, UK
"Standardisation and entry strategies in internationalisation - Dr Maktoba **Omar**, Coventry University, UK

Q & A

Food for Thought – Reflections on the Food Supply Chain and Cities"

Jonathan Liu, Regent's University London, UK

Perhaps there is no better example of the impact of how food and culture can shape a city than London's China Town. London's China Town today, and in many respect the city of London is seen as one of the best cities in the world for Chinese food. Over the last four to five decades, London's China Town at Leicester Square has grown from a few shops to more 80 restaurants and is the hub of Chinese culture in Britain. In 2015, 36.1 million overseas visitors came to the UK and spent £22.1 billion. These figures represent a 5% increase in volume and 1% (nominal) increase in value compared with 2014. London accounts for 54% of all inbound visitor spend, the rest of England 34%, Scotland 8% and Wales 2%. Visit Britain (2016). In 2012, School Food Trust found that learning to cook improves student's recognition of healthier foods and the desire to eat them. 1 in 3 children in the UK are overweight by the age of 9. UK Government's strategy to tackle obesity is to promote healthy cooking in schools. In 2014 cooking lessons became compulsory to all children up to the age of 14. The presentation centres on two projects, the British Chinese Food Culture Project and the Healthy Chinese Cuisine Ambassadors Project, and explores how the change in values and the collaboration between public and private organisations are critical to the growth of destination development in the UK. ***

Doner Kebab taking over the UK

Ibrahim Sirkeci (Regent's University London, United Kingdom)

People move, finances move, so does the artefacts and cultures. Remittances literature expanded significantly in the last two decades to cover more of what we refer to as social remittances. Social remittances refer to often intangible elements, cultural artefacts, habits, opinions, attitudes, beliefs, values transferred by migrants from destination countries to their home countries. Through studies on migrant remittances, we know that even in terms of financial transfers, remittances operate in corridors and in a two-way fashion. One third of remittances are sent to countries which are called "advanced economies". United Kingdom, Germany, France are among the top remittance receiving countries as well as leading the table of sending countries. In this paper, I explore the ways in which social remittances change the foodscapes of destination countries with particular reference to Doner Kebab in the United Kingdom. Until two decades ago, Doner Kebab was an exquisite meal you would enjoy when holidaying in Turkey or if you happen to be in that cosy corner of North London. Nevertheless, in 2010s Britain, it became a leading fast food, particularly when it comes to what to eat after a night out. One may find an outlet selling doner kebab literally in every city, every town, every neighbourhood, every village in Britain. Multiple forces were in play in the making of Doner Kebab a British national food. 1) practicality of the food itself, 2) growing number of immigrants from Turkey arriving in Britain, 3) labour market disadvantages immigrants face, 4) asylum dispersal policies of the 1990s and 2000s, 5) declining incentives making small shops not viable economically, and 6) increasing number of British tourists visiting Turkey.

***

SESSION 1 – Food and identity of places

	Rectorate Hall
Chair	**Ibrahim Sirkeci, Regent's University London, UK**
	Nutrition and food in the Green City - **Paolo Corvo**
	Food & wine tourism and urban local development - **Gabriele Di Francesco**
	Taste and dignity in refugee camps: desert foods versus food aid in Sahrawi refugee camps of southwest Algeria - **Gabriele Volpato**
	Balancing act: identity and otherness among Latin American immigrants and their food practices - **Paulette K. Schuster**

Nutrition and food in the Green City
Paolo Corvo (University of Gastronomic Sciences, Italy)

Food is a significant aspect of the dimension of life quality and of any proposal for a green city: after having solved the problem of finding food, it has become an aesthetic pleasure, an essential element of living well. In the green city the farmer markets are spreading increasingly. They are markets for the farmers who bring their products into the city to be sold, thereby becoming from growers and producers to retailers. Recently the growing success of the Earth Markets displays citizens' desire for quality and genuine food such as fruits, vegetables, meat, cheese. The dissemination and development of farmer market are chiefly due to the awareness that it is necessary to establish a relationship between producers and consumers, in order to have healthy and genuine products, energy saving and a lower environmental impact. Another interesting aspect of the relationship between the green city and nutrition is the dissemination of urban gardens, which provide the cultivation of fruit and vegetables and the production of jams and preserves, the development of agricultural activities in the heart of the green city. Throughout history, the city has always had spaces for agricultural production; today these spaces are limited to the peri-urban area and they are often under the threat of overbuilding and urbanisation. In recent years this risk seems to be reduced both because of the presence of a greater awareness among the citizens about the importance of urban gardens, and because of the economic crisis so that these forms of production have been appreciated, representing a saving in food costs. This phenomenon occurs both at the individual level (even among managers and professionals), with the use of all possible spaces (gardens, terraces, balconies, etc.) and at the public level, with the municipal authorities that have created websites dedicated to cultivation. Sometimes these urban gardens are created in degraded areas, hence playing also a key role in the redevelopment of the territory and in the dissemination of a new sociality.

***

Food & wine tourism and urban local development

Gabriele Di Francesco (Università degli Studi G. D'annunzio, Italy)

Food & wine tourism in Italy is characterized by the reference to natural foods and to the history of the cities. For most of the foods the bond with the territories and especially with the cities was and is crucial. Always food, typically produced in family businesses, have the same name of the cities, as if the city was the real corporate brand of taste. This city brand is often copied in many countries of the world to product industrial supplies that have a wide commercial distribution. These products are impossible to reproduce. They are the result of the combination of local products, craft skills, bonds with legendary or real historical events. The reflection on the food&wine tourism and urban development, comes from these assumptions. With a socio-anthropological approach, some methods and qualitative techniques were used, as the historical comparative method, document analysis and participant observation. These methods were applied to investigate three different Italian towns that gave the name to three foods: Marino, with the wine festival, Fabriano with its production of salami and Ascoli Piceno with the production of the Ascoli olive. The Marino Grape Festival is based on legendary events, on the presence of ancient vineyards, on the representation in the style of 1500s square machines. In Fabriano is produced a famous salami dates back to medieval times, reproduced in paintings and frescoes and handed down to us with a disciplinary unchanged. Ascoli Piceno has given its name to a prized food preparation called Oliva Ascolana. Marino has thousands of visitors every year to drink and buy wine and to participate in the grape and wine festivals. Fabriano has a tourism that seeks the history, architecture, art and the taste of his salami. The Ascoli olive stuffed with meat and spices is great tourist vehicle to Ascoli Piceno.

***

Taste and dignity in refugee camps: desert foods versus food aid in Sahrawi refugee camps of southwest Algeria
Gabriele Volpato (University of Gastronomic Sciences, Italy)

Civil war in the countries and forced migration of local community, adverse effects brought about by the war and adaptation problems in the countries migrated to affect physical, psychological, social, economic and cultural developments of the individuals' at all ecological levels. When all such unfavorable effects are considered, the age, gender and other characteristics of an individual cause level of the impact of the migration and war on the individual to increase. The individuals who essentially need to be protected from the war and migration are the women, children and elderly people. The people of Somali in Sub-Saharan Africa have been struggling against domestic disturbances and war for the last 25 years. Due to insufficient institutional state structure in Somali, unfounded civil peace and piracy, the community was forced to migrate and they requested asylum to Turkey by 1999. In 2009, they settled in Isparta province, which was designated as one of the "satellite town for refugees". That there are Somalian children migrated to Turkey with or without any company makes important that analyzing and investigating experiences of those children. Therefore, it is of great critical importance that the problems encountered by the children during the war and migration and discovering adaptation problems in the countries migrated. The study is a qualitative one to be carried out with the aim of revealing experiences of the children in terms of migration, adaptation problems in the countries migrated and being an immigrant or asylum seeker in a war environment. Data for the study will be collected through snowball sampling. Children will be interviewed face to face by using semi-structured interview forms for the stories of the children and hence it will contribute to psycho-social and social work intervention to be provided for asylum seeker children.

***

Balancing act: identity and otherness among Latin American immigrants and their food practices

Paulette K. Schuster (AMLAT, The Open University of Israel, Hebrew University of Jerusalem, Israel)

This study deals with the identity construction of Latin American immigrants in Israel through their food practices. Food is a basic symbolic element connecting cultural perceptions and experiences. It is also an important element in the maintenance of personal ties with their home countries and a cohesive factor in the construction of a new identity in Israel, their adopted homeland, Food practices encode tacit information and non-verbal cues that are integral parts of an individual's relationship with different social groups. In this case, we will recruit participants from a virtual group formed in the social media of Latin American women living in Israel. The basic assumption of this study posits that certain communication systems are set in motion around food events in various social contexts pertaining to different national or local cuisines and culinary customs. Their meaning, significance and modifications and how they are framed are to be explored in this paper. This study focuses on the adaptation and acculturation process because it is then that immigrants are faced with an interesting duality of reconstructing their cultural perceptions to either fit the existing national collective ethos or create a new reality. In this study, the main objective is to compare two different immigrant groups: Jewish and non-Jewish women from Latin America Who came to Israel during the last ten years. The comparative nature of the research will reveal marked differences between ethnic, religious and cultural elements that reflect coping strategies manifested in cultural production of food and its representation in two distinct domains: private and public. In the former, it is illustrated within the family and home and how they connect or clash with the former in the form of consumption in the street. Combining cultural studies and discourse analysis, this paper offers fresh insight into new models of food practices and reproductions. The article's contribution to new food research lies in its ability to shed light on how intergenerational and interreligious discourses are blurred while food practices and traditions are embedded in a new Israeli identity.

***

SESSION 2 – Food mobility & cityscape - everyday life, rituals, experiences, street food, foodscapes

	Rectorate Hall
Chair	**Paolo Corvo, University of Gastronomic Sciences, Italy**
	Coffeescape of the City: Istanbul and London - **Nihal Bursa, Mine Galip Koca**
	Visit Hagia Sophia while having a dürüm and a glass of frothy ayran: the growing trend of experiencing the local food culture of a city - **Banu Ozden**
	Aspiring 'Turkishness' in Belgium through food consumption: Cases of Simit Sarayı, Kahve Dünyası and Güllüoglu – **Saliha Ozdemir**
	The budding aromas from taco trucks: taste and space in Austin, Texas - **Robert D. Lemon**
	Feeding the dead - the symbolic meals in the Romanian funeral ritual – **Stiniguta-Laslo Ella**

Coffeescape of the City: Istanbul and London
Nihal Bursa, Mine Galip Koca (Beykent University, Turkey)

This article proposes to examine how the culture of coffee drinking influences the cityscape while focusing on Istanbul and London as the imperial capitals of the period. Coffee is a delightful part of our everyday life; it is a sociable drink; it defines our perception of the space and the way to socialize, then it becomes a powerful agent in marketing and branding places. In that respect, coffeescape of London in the mid-17th century stands as a remarkable example. The first coffeehouses in London and many others in Europe were established by the people having some level of connections with the Ottoman world. The London coffeehouses first opened in the mid-17th century were all marking as the land of coffee culture, the Ottoman Empire; they were signifying the Turks; coffeehouses with Turkish names, coffee tokens with a Turkish figure, waiters wearing turban. It can be defined as staging cof-fee as a Turkish beverage. Coffee as a beverage of Turks was like a brand. On the other hand, the coffeescape of Istanbul, as an excellent exemplary of the cities like, Bosnia, Jerusalem, Cairo, Belgrade, Kosova, etc. will be examined in this study. While doing this, it will also be discussed the promotion of a new and selective coffee drinker by the marketing strategies which start to mediate our relationship with coffee. For instance, in Istanbul, there's a coffee festival organized once in a year. It provides vivid scenes of coffee culture from the accounts of Western traveller to the third wave coffee today. Thus, how coffee recently defines the cityscape of Istanbul once being one of the homelands of the turban wearing Turkish figure on the British coffee token will also be discussed.

***

Visit Hagia Sophia while having a dürüm and a glass of frothy ayran: the growing trend of experiencing the local food culture of a city
Banu Ozden (YESAM, Turkey)

Alternative tourism has been an important aspect of travelling within the last decade for avid travellers who are actually looking to get involved in a local culture, and gain new experiences. Turkey has been one of those destinations where the food culture has played an important role. According to the recent reports published by TURSAB, 88.2% of the travellers choose the destination based on food. This also affects the amount of money spent when visiting other cities. In Turkey, the numbers from 2014 shows that this equals to about one-fifth of the total money tourists spend during their visit to Turkey. As the world becomes our oyster and travelling is simplified thanks to technology, the simple acts of sight-seeing, visiting the popular museums, watching a concert will not suffice unless accompanied by local tastes. The term "local" here really stands for the most authentic, most out of the beaten path and most un-touristy eating experiences. Nutrition is the most basic need for all living things. For societies; nutrition, in addition to being a physical need, is also a behavior which reflects the level of cultural development and taste. Every society has their own food culture based on geographical, ecological, economic characteristic features and the historical process. However, some societies have taken the raw materials provided by nature and learned to process them to such an extent that they have taken their food cultures beyond the meeting of a need and imbued them with an esthetic value and turned them into an artform. Turkey and Turkish culture are one of those societies mentioned above, given the vast geography that the Turks have lived on and the long history. When one talks about Turkish cuisine, the term should be understood as the totality of foods and beverages which provide nutrition to the people living in Turkey, the ways of preparing and preserving them; techniques, equipment and utensils required for this, eating manners and all the practices and beliefs which are developed around this cuisine. When speaking of food experiences Turkey has a lot to offer to those who are visiting with food in mind, including the making and the rituals that go along with it. This paper will reveal the aspects of food experiences of Turkey and how it is naturally embedded into the daily lives of the locals and how this can be experienced by the travellers who are looking to taste the dishes of Turkey in the most genuine sense.

   ***

Aspiring 'Turkishness' in Belgium through food consumption: cases of Simit Sarayı, Kahve Dünyası and Güllüoğlu

Saliha Ozdemir (KU Leuven, Belgium)

This paper discusses the emerging consumption of Turkish brands by second generation Europeans of Turkish provenance within the framework of the food, 'national identity' (Brightwell 2012; Costa &Bestio 2011; Hirsh & Tene 2013; Hsu & Pang 2013; Wilk 2002) and the aspiration for Turkish leisure and lifestyle and the nexus taste/synesthesia (Sutton 2001; Pang 2015). It is based on ethnographic findings collected in three locations: Simit Sarayı (bakery chain) in Rotterdam, Güllüoglu (patisserie chain) in Brussels and Kahve Dünyası (coffeehouse chain) in London. These high-end shops are subsidiaries of well-entrenched Turkish brands in Turkey, which have found their way to posh and upscale quarters of European capitals instead of locating them in disadvantaged ethnic neighborhoods in these cities. First, a historical overview is provided highlighting the search for Turkish food and the rise of ethnic food-scape created by migrants of Turkish provenance since the start of their migration story. Second, their taste for consuming Turkish brands developed in global Turkey, manifested in specific consumption patterns and performances will be explored both at the level of symbolic consumption as well at the physiological dimension of specific taste preferences. The symbolic dimension refers to the sociability and celebration of a 'global' Turkish lifestyle. An exploration of the reception of carefully culturally curated 'Turkish' brands lends to a better understanding of how 'Turkishness' as a discursive category is being enacted, articulated, consumed and constructed by local consumers of Turkish provenance in specific social-commercial spaces in European cities. The article argues that the emergence of these upscale businesses both substantiates as well as supports the notion of global consumption of 'Turkish lifestyle' outside of Turkey, and at the same time fosters a shift of the social spaces of Turkish migrants breaking out from poor ethnic neighborhoods into more mainstream neighborhoods of the city.

***

The budding aromas from taco trucks: taste and space in Austin, Texas

Robert D. Lemon (The University of Texas at Austin, United States)

This paper evaluates how taste preferences produce space in Austin, Texas. Austin is a booming city. Indeed, it has been the fastest growing metro area in the United States for the past 10 to 20 years. It is also renowned for its evolving and enthralling food truck scene. Food trucks of all sorts spring up throughout the city.

Some of the more innovative foods stem from gourmet trucks. And these trucks often become symbolic capital that spur gentrification. Other trucks, such as the traditional taco truck, are ensconced in marginalized neighborhoods. They feed the working masses of Mexicans who flock to Austin to find work. Certainly, the gourmet truck vendors experiment with food flavors; however, taco truck entrepreneurs are innovative as well. The taco truck cooks must certainly modify their food to accommodate Austin's shifting demographics. To this end, I argue Austin's landscape transformation can be examined through cooking practices. This paper takes a close look at how immigrant cooks negotiate social spaces through the foods they make. In so doing, I interviewed two traditional taco truck owners about how they decide what to cook based on the social spaces in which they park their trucks. Surprisingly, their subtle choices reflect the changing culture and budding taste preferences of the city's residents.

***

Feeding the dead – the symbolic meals in the Romanian funeral ritual
Stiniguta-Laslo Ella (Babes-Bolyai University of Cluj-Napoca, Romania)

Funeral meals are part of the ritual for almost every community around the world, in different eras and for multiple purposes, one of which is the commensality with the dead. The Romanian tradition states that the family must provide free food for the relatives, neighbours and especially for the poor when a member dies. So, feeding other people means feeding the dead, the food offerings for the poor actually being made for the soul of the dead, helping him to pass the seven, twelve or twenty-four "borders of the sky" and to arrive peacefully in Heaven. Moreover, not being able to keep the tradition is believed to bring misfortune for the dead (he or she will not have an easy journey to paradise or will never go there) but also for the family too (they will not have a proper burial either, leading to an eternal sufferance in Hell). The aim of my paper is to describe the different types of alms and food gifts and to establish which of them have the function of commensality and which of separation. Also, I will try to identify the multiple stages, the special dishes and foods used in the burial ritual with their symbolical significance, the specific sayings and religious gestures that accompany the food offerings.

SESSION 3 – Food as culture – heritage, identity, myths, narratives

	Rectorate Hall
Chair	**Evinç Doğan, University of Belgrade, Serbia**
	Culinary heritage as a branding, bragging and bracing vehicle: GAP experience in Turkey – **Aylin Öney Tan**
	Lyon - UNESCO Creative City of Gastronomy? – **Cecilia Avelino Barbosa**
	The role of periurban agricultural areas in the preservation and valorization of local culture and identity through food heritage in Barcelona – **Mercè Civera Pérez**
	Is Serbian cuisine a national myth? – **Ana Veljkovic, Stefan Milutinovic, Vojin Simunovic**
	Pork and Prejudice or in the Quest for the Taste of Belgrade – **Tamara Ognjevic**

Culinary heritage as a branding, bragging and bracing vehicle: GAP experience in Turkey

Aylin Öney Tan (Food Columnist, Researcher, Consultant, Turkey)

Claiming the nationality of certain foods is an inevitable act of "patriotism"; especially so because food does not recognize any boundary-let alone that of the nation-states. Spatiality of food is not determined by the political boundaries. The phenomenon of vying for the national origins of food occurs in almost every neighbouring country in the Balkans and the Middle East; verbal battles rage on between Greece, Bulgaria and Turkey over the ownership of yogurt in the Balkans front; while the debate over best lahmacun, and kebab remains as inter-city battle within Turkey itself. Meanwhile, a sweet teeth debate digs into the nationality of baklava spread over a wide geographical arch starting from the Balkans to the Middle East. In fact, all these cultures share not only the recent Ottoman past, but also a number of overlapping civilisations with complex structures spanning throughout the ages. When it comes to culinary practices it is definitely the local culinary cultures and geography that rules; retaining an impact far beyond ethnic or religious backgrounds. Nevertheless, in our present-day world everyone tries to find their share in global economy, a reference to culinary heritage becomes a tool for branding cities and products. Local cuisines and products are utilized as a tool for bragging about nationalistic values, resulting in inter-city or even district battles over a single dish; but culinary heritage also provides a chance for bracing opportunities with regards to raising opportunities for sustainable livelihood and preservation of local produce. With this analytical framework in the background, this paper will be based on my observations in South East Anatolia over the course last two decades, especially in Gaziantep, recently designated as a Gastronomy City in the UNESCO Creative Cities Network. I have worked extensively in the area for international cultural heritage projects first as an architectural conservation expert, and subsequently as a food writer and researcher, and finally as the gastronomy consultant for the GAP Tourism and Branding Project. Combining my multiple professional fields of study, I will be discussing my observations, debating various aspects of culinary heritage, now seen as a treasure to promote tourism.

***

Lyon - Unesco Creative City of Gastronomy?

Cecilia Avelino Barbosa (Universidade Nova de Lisboa, Portugal)

The output for the XXI century problems of cities seems to be the use of creativity applied to the reorganization of the territory. Many cities call themselves Creative in order to attract international investment, the catalyst of competition between territories has been marketing places. In order to analyze these concepts in the international promotion of a city, we turn our case study for the city of Lyon, France. This territorial clipping was observed for seven months by this researcher, provided participant observer with the central purpose of examining the territorial marketing techniques Only Lyon program and realize the consequences of these actions to the imagination of tourists and locals, as well as for the economic development of the city. Among the objectives we seek to identify the main features of a creative city, and what influence this label set up by UNESCO prints the daily lives of local residents. As methodological procedure, we take into account the dynamics of the city, their daily lives and cultural offer, keeping a first spontaneous contact with the Only Lyon brand to then define reading strategies such as: identify strategies aimed at improving the service offered, attracting companies and professionals, promoting the city in an international context and to maintain the quality of life of residents. We had also been made semi-structured interviews with the communication department of cultural centers, city dwellers and tourists. Upon completion of the analysis, we see the positive results of marketing attitude adopted by that mark, responsible for making Lyon the Creative City of the Gastronomy in the eyes of locals and tourists. On the other hand, we also observed an absence in the promotion of activities for the Digital Arts, curiously the field that led Lyon to obtain the title of Creative City by UNESCO.

 ***

The role of periurban agricultural areas in the preservation and valorization of local culture and identity through food heritage in Barcelona

Mercè Civera Pérez (Campus CETT-UB, Spain)

Barcelona is a consolidated urban tourism destination. When it comes to the city's brand image, it is widely associated with creativity, innovation, culture, excellent gastronomy, sustainability and high quality of life. In fact, Barcelona ranks first smart city in Spain and fourth in Europe. Within the framework of smart, sustainable destinations, the Town Council focuses on building an image of Barcelona as an environmentally committed city, caring for biodiversity and fostering green economy; issues which revolve aroud the four key pillars of sustainability. This paper aims at analyzing the role played by Barcelona's two peri-urban agricultural areas: Parc Agrari del Baix Llobregat and Consorci de Gàllecs in the preservation and valorisation of local food culture and in raising environmental awareness. The methodology includes literary review related to food tourism and sustainable destinations, analysis of projects peri-urban agricultural areas are engaged in, qualitative techniques such as in-depth interviews with chefs and the managers of both agricultural spaces and quantitative techniques with surveys to locals and tourists. The most outstanding findings reveal that these farmlands comply with the principles of sustainability: related to Slow Food, they carry out actions for the promotion of the local product through markets, food events, or farm tours and are actively committed with environmental education programs. Regarding the safeguard of biodiversity, some native species and seeds have been recovered and awarded with labels to garantee the product quality, origin and seasonality or local farmers' know how. The findings also demonstrate that the impact of their actions and the scope of knowledge dissemination is not as significant as it was expected. We can conclude that periurban agricultural areas can become an excellent tool for the safeguard of local food and culture playing an important role in terms of sustainable development. Besides, with the implementation of appropriate strategies, the agricultural and tourism sectors can be integrated in order to generate more resources for the region's development.

    ***

Is Serbian cuisine a national myth?

Ana Veljkovic, Stefan Milutinovic, Vojin Simunovic (Central and East European Studies at the University of Glasgow, United Kingdom; Political Science at Corvinus University of Budapest, Hungary)

Almost every country in the world has its national cuisine. The process of emergence of a national cuisine is very complex, and it includes many historical, symbolic, and ideological factors, especially considering that today cuisine has become one of the key parts of the national identity of a country. When being asked to describe their own cuisine, most people will reply in superlatives, often without questioning its authenticity. However, recent scholarship and research claim that the idea of national cuisine is a myth, often accompanied by the process of nation-state formation. The main aim of this paper is to conduct an analysis of the Serbian cuisine in this light, and try to answer the question of how authentic and "Serbian" is Serbian cuisine in the context of the modern Serbian state, and Serbian national identity. For this purpose, we have chosen one of the most widely used cookbooks – Patin Kuvar (Pata's cookbook), published in 1939, by one of the first culinary educated women in Serbia, while focusing on the elements of the Ottoman-Turkish heritage inherent in this book. The

Ottoman-Turkish elements have not been chosen by accident. Centuries of Ottoman rule in Serbia have created a huge discourse based on the idea of Turks as the "enemies", which has become a strong part of the national identity of many Serbs, starting from 19th century when Serbia gained independence from the Ottoman Empire. In this sense, the analysis of Pata's cookbook gives out results that can even be described as "shocking". The Ottoman heritage, which is also present in today's Turkey, is very strong, and it raises questions related to the authenticity and "Serbianness" of the Serbian cuisine, especially in relation to the national identity of Serbs, and the existing discourse around it.

***

Pork and prejudice or in the quest for the taste of Belgrade
Tamara Ognjevic (Artis Center, Serbia)

Belgrade is a true gastronomic Babylon, the point of meeting, permeating and reshaping of the most diverse culinary influences. On the one hand it provides the city with interesting and challenging potentials while also making it difficult to define an authentic gastronomic identity. What is actually a typical taste of Belgrade and is it possible to brand Serbian capital in terms of food as suggested within modern trends in tourism? This paper, based on the research of gastronomic heritage of Belgrade from the late Middle Ages to the beginning of the new millennium considers, interalia, the most common mistakes in understanding and placing national specialties in the tourist offer of Serbia, as well as the untapped potential offered due to synthesis of the cultural, creative and gastronomic tourism in the cities that are still in the proces of creating their own foodscapes.

***

SESSION 4 – Food as brand - image and identity of place perceived through food

	Rectorate Hall
Chair	**Goran Petkovic, University of Belgrade, Serbia**
	The Role of Cuisines in the Construction of Nation Brand: Turkey's Gastro Hunt Project – **Gaye Aslı Sancar**
	Cravings for Morality: Why ethically labeled food tastes better? - **Iskra Herak**
	Serbia's Brand Positioning through Food: Case of Expo Milano 2015 – **Evinç Doğan, Goran Petkovic**
	Food in tourism and social eating trend: An exploratory study of the Italian expats' role in promoting the gastronomic made in Italy - **Alessandra Campanari, Alessio Cavicchi**
	Investigating Thessalonian Culinary Landscapes: As a Way to Develop an Alternative Image of the City as a Travel Destination – **George Chatzinakos**

The Role of Cuisines in the Construction of Nation Brand: Turkey's Gastro Hunt Project

Gaye Aslı Sancar (Galatasaray University, Turkey)

A culture's cuisine and an interest to the cuisine play an important role choosing travel destinations. Because of Italy's pizza and pasta, the French's onion soup, Spain's paella and Greece's many different dishes, in common with

Turkey, tourists prefer to travel such countries more often. In this sense, countries take advantages of their cuisines to attract tourists. Although it initially seems promotion of food culture is intended to appeal many tourists, its primary objective is to support nation brand in the long terms. The so-called culinary diplomacy or gastro-diplomacy, as another newly introduced concept to the literature, serve to foreign policies of countries as well and, when necessary, it even emerges in diplomatic dinners which significant issues are on the table. The use of food as a way to promote nation brand, to put another way, is constructing brand promise for countries. In this respect, the Turkish dishes are a promising experience for tourists. The starting point of the study is the role of food cultures in nation brand. In this context, Turkey's Gastro Hunt Project launched in 2014 will be analyzed. Specifically, answers will be sought to the following questions: Did Turkey's Gastro Hunt Project deliver the right messages to the right target audience? How were social media reactions towards the Gastro Hunt Project?

***

Cravings for Morality: Why ethically labeled food tastes better?

Iskra Herak (Université Catholique de Louvain, Belgium)

For food consumption, taste and price are two criteria of outmost importance, however, it seems that ethical issues concerning the food production and/or distribution are beginning to take a noteworthy spot as well (SoilAssociation, 2010, European Commission,2012; Fair Trade International, 2012). Having in mind that this kind of nutrition is frequently pricy, many started to question what lies behind this trend, especially since one couldn't argue that there has been an increase in economic standard of overall population. So far, studies revealed that intentions to buy organic (Arvola et al., 2008) and fair trade (Shaw & Shiu, 2002) food are predicted by moral considerations such as the desire to preserve the environment and helping producers from developing countries. Although worthy of appreciation, this kind of altruistic behavior doesn't seem to be a sufficient explanation and the only underlying cause since growth rates of other pro-environmental behaviors (e.g. recycling) haven't been noted (Defra, 2011). Bratanova, Kervyn and Klein (2015) tackled this question and proposed that the superior subjective gustatory experience of ethically branded food may complement the role of morality in sustaining and boosting consumers 'cravings' for it. Authors tested first whether food of ethical origin is experienced as subjectively tastier compared to food of conventional or unethical origin. Furthermore, they postulated that its subjectively superior taste may act as a reward mechanism, reinforcing subsequent buying intentions and willingness to pay a higher price. Series of studies that involved one large scale international survey, three experimental studies involving actual food consumption of different type of ethical origin (organic, fair trade and locally produced), confirmed these assumptions.

***

Serbia's Brand Positioning through Food: Case of Expo Milano 2015

Evinç Doğan, Goran Petkovic (University of Belgrade, Serbia)

Food and gastronomic values of a country are distinguished assets in marketing places. The aim of this research is exploring how Serbia rebrands itself through promoting the local food and culture. The key concepts for this research originate from the literature in place marketing and branding. We focus on the country's gastronomic offer shaping people's perceptions about that particular place and its culture. EXPO Milano 2015 is the case for analyzing the ways in which Serbia's brand image is represented and communicated through values, narratives and manifestations. Accordingly, semiotics is adopted for analyzing the data, which builds on three levels: axiological, narrative and discursive. Content analysis is used as a supportive method to infer meanings from codes and to determine emerging themes overarching the units of meaning. The tourism marketing strategy of The National Tourism Organization of Serbia (TOS) is scrutinized, while the case of EXPO constitutes the example of real life event to see if the messages are consistent in favor of the marketing communications to achieve desired outcomes. In doing so, the data collected during the three months field study period in Milano (May-July 2015) are evaluated together with the official promotion materials by TOS in an answer to the question if the branding strategies, goals and messages follow the same line or differ from each other. Consequently, the analysis results show, how the country branding strategy of Serbia is handled in terms of the impact on the perceptions with a focus on food as a tourist attraction. The research is valuable for place-marketers, strategists, governments, and scholars from different fields of academia.

***

Food in tourism and social eating trend: An exploratory study of the Italian expats' role in promoting the gastronomic made in Italy

Alessandra Campanari, Alessio Cavicchi
(University of Macerata, Italy)

Nowadays, the focus of the tourism industry has shifted from mass to niche and the experience economy (Pine, Gilmore, 1998) has favoured a new interest in gastronomic tourism, where tourists seek sensory experiences and food offers the chance to explore all five senses (Santini et al., 2011). This trend has developed a new concept inside the sharing economy called *social eating* that consist in eating at others' home to directly experience the cultural heritage of the hosting country. In this context Italy, where food is one of the main attractions for tourists, can represent a significant case study to explore the dimensions of culinary tourism. Plus, if we consider that Italians have always had a straightforward relationship with food as cultural identity, it is even more interesting to analyze the role of Italian expats in promoting the gastronomic Made in Italy abroad. Thus this study wants to examine how social eating can provide alternative opportunities to explore the culinary tourism experience and analyze if and to what extent Italian expats can promote an authentic image of Italy abroad. (i) Promotion of food tourism inside the social eating trend, (ii) the

connection between Italian expats and Italian
food identity in the promotion of the
gastronomic Made in Italy abroad. A mixed
method approach, with qualitative research (semi-
structured open-ended interviews) with 20 key
informants (Italian expats currently participating
to social eating initiatives) and a survey
administered to hosts of social eating initiatives in
Italy. Analysis of the literature demonstrated how
food became an important touristic attraction. In
this context, social eating platforms can boost the
promotion of traditional recipes and can re-
educate the new generations of Italian families
emigrated abroad from late 19th century to the
first half of 20th century.

***

Investigating Thessalonian culinary landscapes: as a way to develop an alternative image of the city as a travel destination

George Chatzinakos (Manchester Metropolitan
University, United Kingdom)

The project seeks to conceptualize the way
Thessaloniki is promoting alternative forms of
tourism such as culinary tourism, while
supporting and/or building upon local networks;
engaging and co-creating an urban experience
with its citizens and visitors. A long-term aim of
this research is to suggest a framework that can
be used as a strategic planning tool for the
promotion of culinary tourism in Thessaloniki;

developing an alternative image of the city as a culinary destination. The start point of the research was to investigate the role of Thessaloniki Food Festival, an event which aims in promoting and upgrading local gastronomy and establishing the city as a target for culinary tourism. The research tried to provide a lens through which the culinary culture of Thessaloniki, can be used as strategic pillar for stimulating a sustainable way of 'consuming' and promoting the city's identity. In order to access and understand how the experiences and the interaction of different urban actors, fashion Thessaloniki' urban fabric and its culinary identity, a qualitative approach was considered more appropriate. Through semi-structured interviews I approached 15 different stakeholders that in one way or another are associated with the culinary landscape of the city. Thus, additional data was provided through netnography. In this direction (objectives), the research tried to identify what is going on in the city in terms of culinary tourism, understand some basic cultural elements regarding Thessalonian gastronomic identity, and locate the challenges the city is facing when it comes to the development of culinary resources in order the last to be used for the promotion of culinary tourism.

***

Author Index

www.transnationalmarket.com
www.tplondon.com/bordercrossing
www.tplondon.com

TRANSNATIONAL
MARKETING
JOURNAL
ISSN: 2041-4684
e-ISSN: 2041-4692

Volume 4
Number 1
May 2016

TRANSNATIONAL PRESS LONDON

www.transnationalmarket.com

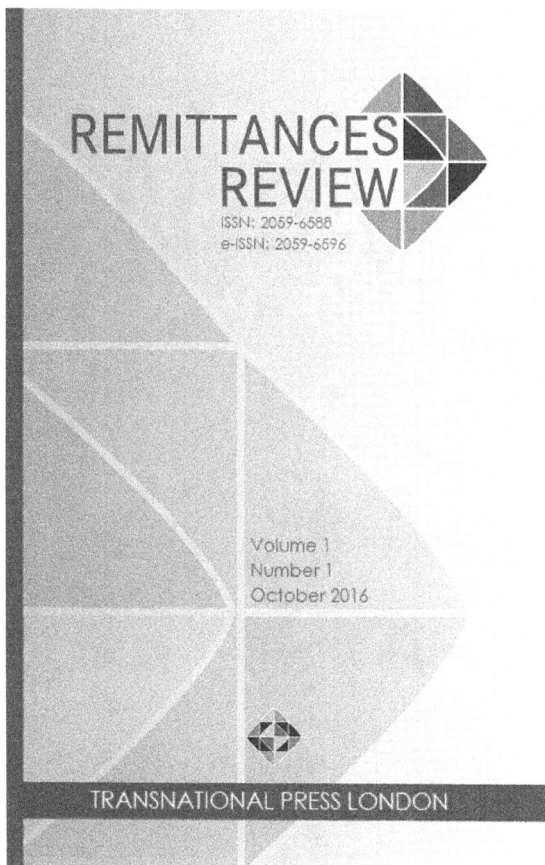

REMITTANCES
REVIEW

ISSN: 2059-6588
e-ISSN: 2059-6596

Volume 1
Number 1
October 2016

TRANSNATIONAL PRESS LONDON

www.tplondon.com/rem

IMAGE OF
ISTANBUL
IMPACT OF ECOC 2010 ON
THE CITY IMAGE

Evinç DOĞAN

MANAGEMENT SERIES BY TRANSNATIONAL PRESS LONDON

www.tplondon.com/istanbulimage

NOTES:

NOTES:

NOTES:

NOTES:

NOTES:

NOTES:

NOTES:

NOTES: